John Rettig

The Fall of Babylon

John Rettig

The Fall of Babylon

ISBN/EAN: 9783337308742

Printed in Europe, USA, Canada, Australia, Japan

Cover: Foto ©ninafisch / pixelio.de

More available books at **www.hansebooks.com**

A HISTORICAL, BIBLICAL and SPECTACULAR DRAMA.

o o o o o o o o o o o

PRODUCED UNDER THE IMMEDIATE SUPERVISION AND MANAGEMENT OF THE
BOARD OF CONSTRUCTION OF THE

Order of Cincinnatus.

JNO. R. MOSBY, Chairman.   *T. W. GRAYDON, Vice-Chairman.*   *A. S. BERRY, Vice-Chairman.*

GEO. A. VANDERGRIFT, Acting Secretary and Treasurer.   *R. A. W. BRUEHL, Financial Secretary*

JAMES O'KANE.   *GEO. T. STERRETT.*   *W. L. ROBINSON.*

A. PLUEMER.   *W. B. SMITH.*   *J. P. LOVE.*   *GEORGE ILSEN*

o o o o o o o o o o o

On the CAMPUS, Foot of Bank St.

COMMENCING JULY 23, 1888.

PERFORMANCE BEGINS AT 8.15 P. M.

*General Ticket Office, Big Four R. R. and Kankakee Line Ticket Office, N. W. Cor.
Fourth and Walnut Streets.   Address all communications to Maj.
Geo. A. Vandergrift, Burnet House, Cincinnati.*

A BRIEF DESCRIPTION

—— OF THE ——

City of Babylon,

600 Years before the Christian Era.

BABYLON, AN ANCIENT CITY of Assyria, in what is now Turkey in Asia, lying on the banks of the River Euphrates, about 200 miles from the Persian Gulf.

The sacred historian gives us few particulars of the migrations of the human race after Noah and his family left the Ark. One body of them journeyed east to the land of Shinar, which is supposed to be Chaldea. Here they undertook a singular project,—that of building a city and tower, "whose top might reach heaven." It is generally understood that Babylon was afterwards built on this spot.

Various motives have been assigned for this enterprise. On this point, however, we can offer little except conjecture. The only distinct information we have in relation to it is, that the design was displeasing to the Almighty, and to prevent its completion, He "confounded their speech, so that they left off to build the city" and were dispersed over the face of the earth. In commemoration of this remarkable event, the place was called *Babel*, meaning in the Chaldean, "The gate of (the highest) God," but the Hebrew form is explained by *Balel*, (or Bilbel) to confound, in allusion to the confounding of tongues consequent on the building of the Tower of Babel.

At the time of the fall of the first Assyrian empire which occurred about 876 *B. C.*, three considerable kingdoms were formed, one of which was that of the Assyrians of Babylon and known as *Babylonia*.

Babylon begun its career under Belesis, about 876 *B. C.*, but without calling attention to the names and deeds of the succeeding kings we come to the reign of Nebuchadnezzar about 647 *B. C.*

Nebuchadnezzar having become displeased by the several revolts of the Jews, marched against them with an overwhelming force. Jerusalem was taken and plundered and a large number of its inhabitants were made captives, among whom was the prophet Daniel.

REIGN OF NEBUCHADNEZZAR.

During the reign of Nebuchadnezzar, and for a considerable period before and after, the city of Babylon appears to have been not only the seat of an imperial court, but a station for a vast garrison. The Babylonians carried on an extensive trade in the east with Persia and northern India where they obtained gold, dyestuffs and precious stones. From Candahar and Cashmere, fine wool and shawls, all of this intercourse being maintained by means of caravans.

Babylon owed its chief greatness to Nebuchadnezzar, and there can be no doubt that Babylon, as built by Nebuchadnezzar and captured by Cyrus, was one of the great cities of the world, though of necessity built of perishable materials.

How magnificent must have been the " golden city," the "beauty of the Chaldees' excellency," when complete in all its vast proportions! The accounts given by ancient authors of its magnificence, and its extent, its walls, its riches, and its decorations, appear the creations of Oriental fancy rather than the sober facts of history; and yet these accounts are so circumstantial and so well authenticated, that at least in their great leading features, they may be received as true.

One main source of all this wealth and grandeur was the Euphrates. Its waters, distributed by art and science, by canals and hydraulic machines, over the vast plains, occasioned a fertility such as few lands can boast; while its productions, vegetable and live, rendered the territory of Babylon the store house of the nation.

Again and again did its Nebuchadnezzars and other po-
tentates penetrate to distant lands.   More than once they pil-
laged Jerusalem, and made its people captives; though that
victory proved the ruin of Babylon, when Belshazzar used
the sacred vessels of the Temple to pander to his pride or
his passion.

The description of the city by Herodotus is undoubtedly
the one upon which the greatest reliance can be placed.   Not
only is he the earliest profane writer on the subject, but he is
the only ancient historian that we know to have been there in
person, and that, too, while it was in a state of tolerable
preservation.

According to Herodotus, Babylon was built in the form
of a square, each side of which was 120 stadia in length ; its
circumference being, therefore, 480 stadia or about 55 of
our miles.

It was surrounded by a wall of enormous height and
thickness, outside of which was a vast trench filled with
water, and proportioned in depth and width to the elevation of
the wall.   The earth taken out of the trench was made into
bricks for the construction of the wall.   These were baked
in furnaces, and afterwards cemented by heated bitumen.
Layers of reeds were interposed at regular intervals to make
the mass more homogeneous.   Upon the top, along the edges
of the wall, were constructed buildings of a single chamber, leaving sufficient space between them for a chariot drawn by four
horses to turn around.

Canals were cut out on the east side of the river, above
the city, to prevent any inconvenience from its periodical inun-
dations, occasioned by the melting of the snow in the moun-
tains of Armenia, by conveying the superabundant water into
the river Tigris.   The principal of these was the Naher
Malcha, or Royal Canal.

The streets of the city crossed each other at right angles,
forming squares, each two miles and a quarter in circuit.
The river ran through the city from north to south, and on
each side of the river was a quay of the same thickness as the
wall.

Opposite the ends of the streets leading to the river were
openings in the embankments, with brazen gates, and steps

leading down to the river; and "these gates were open by day, but shut by night." It was by means of these gates, which had been left open, that Cyrus obtained access into the city.

THE HANGING GARDENS.

Nothing however, at Babylon, was more wonderful than the Hanging Gardens, lying along the banks of the river, blooming with fragrant flowers, shaded by a thousand trees, cooled by fountains, whose jeweled waters sparkled in the sunlight, and justly considered one of the "Seven Wonders of the World." Constructed by Nebuchadnezzar, in compliance with a wish of his queen Amytis, who cherished a fond remembrance of elevated groves, such as she had enjoyed on the hills around her native Ecbatana.

For this purpose an artificial mountain was reared, in the form of a square, of four plethra on each side, with terraces rising one above another, to a height overtopping the walls of the city; the ascent from terrace to terrace being by steps ten feet wide.

The floor of each terrace or garden was formed in the following manner : on the tops of the piers was first laid, a pavement of flat stones, 16 feet in length and 4 feet in breadth, over which was a layer of reeds, mixed with a great quantity of bitumen, and this again was covered with two courses of bricks, closely cemented together with plaster ; while over all these were placed thick sheets of lead, on which was laid the earth or mold of the garden. This floorage was designed to retain the moisture of the mold ; and in order to provide a sufficient depth for the largest trees to take firm root, immense hollow piers were built and filled with earth.

PALACE OF NEBUCHADNEZZAR.

At the other end of the bridge stood the superb palace of Nebuchadnezzar, the magnificence of which excited the imagination of all who beheld it, surrounded by a triple wall, whose gates were made of the brass taken from Jerusalem. The inner wall, which was three miles in circumference, was ornamented on one face with delineations of hunting scenes, etc.

Within the triple inclosure rose the palace, which far excelled in magnificence any other in the Empire, and wherein the walls were varnished and adorned with pictures of the

chase, of martial processions and festive scenes; whose apartments were furnished with the carpets of Persia, the silks of Damascus, the jewels of Bokhara, and whose imperial occupant was at once the dread and admiration of all nations.

The walls of the banqueting-hall were covered with mortar and plaster of the finest quality. Here Belshazzar gave that memorable feast to a thousand of his lords, whereat he and his princes, his wives and his concubines, drank wine from the golden and silver vessels which Nebuchadnezzar had taken out of the temple at Jerusalem, and which feast was terminated so abruptly by the ghastly apparition of the fingers of a man's hand, which came forth and wrote on the wall:

"MENE MENE, TEKEL UPHARSIN."

Here Daniel, an eye witness to both, reproved kings, defended his captive brethren, and displayed a devotion to his God which power could not intimidate nor royal favors corrupt.

THE TOWER OF BABEL.

Rising above all other structures was the Tower of Babel, crowned with the statue of Belus made of the finest gold, which shone resplendent in the morning and evening sunlight. How grand must have been that tower when seen in the vastness of it proportions and the fullness of its glory. Commenced by Nimrod, continued by Semiramis, completed by Nebuchadnezzar, it was at once a sanctuary, a mausoleum and an observatory. The ascent was on the exterior, and consisted of broad flights of steps extending from terrace to terrace.

That this is the oldest historic monument known to man is established by the brief and definite statement of Moses: "And it came to pass, as they journeyed from the east that they found a plain in the land of Shinar, and they dwelt there. And they said one to another: 'Go to, let us make brick for stone' "and slime had they for mortar." "And they said: "Go to, let us make a city, and a tower whose top may reach unto heaven: and let us make a name lest we be scattered abroad upon the face of the earth."

What memories are recalled by this structure; the wanderings of the descendants of Noah; the ambition and kingship of Nimrod; the high resolve to build a tower which no flood could submerge; the displeasure of the Lord; the confusion of tongues; the completion of the tower by Nebuchadnezzar.

THE TEMPLE OF BELUS.

Near the tower and within the sacred inclosure was a smaller structure, wherein was a golden statue of Bel or Belus the supreme God of the ancient Chaldeans or Babylonians, around which were large tables and chairs of gold. It was to this God that Nebuchadnezzar dedicated a statue in the plain of Dura, on his return from the Jewish War.

Without the temple was a golden altar, whereon were offered sucklings, while near it was a larger altar for the sacrifice of full-grown animals; and adjoining this temple were apartments for the accommodation of the priests and their attendants.

As the temple of the God Belus, it was the place where were deposited the "gold and silver vessels which Nebuchadnezzar had taken out of the temple which was in Jerusalem." On its summit were probably made, at least in part, those astronomical records, dating back nineteen hundred years before our era.

And the Jews have a tradition that here was imprisoned King Zedekiah; and also that here Nebuchadnezzar was confined within the spacious grounds of the temple when he *"did eat grass as the oxen and his body was wet with the dew of heaven, till his hairs were grown like eagle's feathers and his nails like bird's claws."*

But all this glory was to perish in a night. It did not wane like the moon, it fell like lightning from the heaven. How a city so populous, so wealthy, so magnificent could become a desolation is a fact as interesting as it is true. At the death of Nebuchadnezzar, his son, Evil Merodach, came to the throne, his brief and quiet reign did not exceed two years. Conspiracies followed; usurpers sought the crown and sceptre of Babylon. But the right of succession prevailed, and Nabonadis ascended the throne of his fathers. Unfortunately for him and his kingdom he incurred the displeasure of Cyrus, who marched his victorious army against the imperial city.

THE FALL OF BABYLON.

After Cyrus had spent two whole years before Babylon, without making any progress in the siege, he at last thought of the following stratagem, which put him in possession of it. He was informed that a great annual feast was to be held at

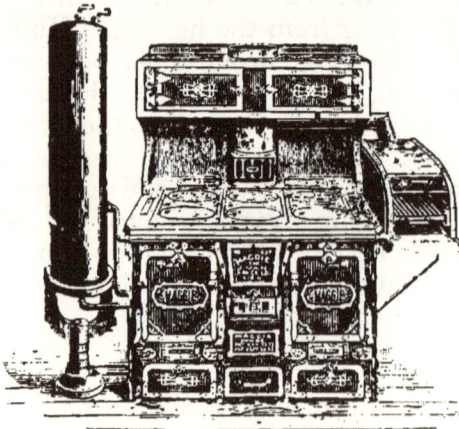

Babylon, and that the inhabitants on that occasion were accustomed to spend the whole night in drinking and debauchery. This he therefore thought a proper time for surprising them ; and accordingly sent a strong detachment to the head of the canal leading to the large lake, with orders, at a certain time, to break down the great bank which was between the lake and the canal, and to turn the whole current into the lake. At the same time he stationed one body of troops at the place where the river entered the city, and another where it came out; ordering them to march in by the bed of the river as soon as they should find it fordable.

On this memorable night, revelry and wild luxury reigned. The prodigious granaries, the stores that seemed exhaustless, men's high hopes, and their spirit of jubilant defiance, all taught Babylon to set its besiegers at naught, and the last King of Babylon was deep in his carouse, and perpetrating sacrilege. When by command of Cyrus, one body of troops under Gobyras, the other under Gadates, finding the gates all left open in consequence of the disorders of that riotous night, penetrated into the very heart of the city. Then followed the scene of hurry, confusion, fire and slaughter which had been foretold by the prophecies of Jeremiah.

In vain did "one host run to meet another, to show the King of Babylon that his city was taken at one end, and that the passages were stopped.' "The mighty men of Babylon forbore to fight; they became as women." "Her princes were made drunk, her wise men, her captains, her rulers, and her mighty men, they slept a perpetual sleep."

"The broad walls of Babylon were utterly broken, and her high gates were burned with fire ; the people labored in vain and the folk in the fire." "In that night was Belshazzar the King of the Chaldeans slain."

Thus was Babylonia reduced to a province of Persia, and the great Empire of Babylon numbered with the things of the past.

Prominent and Attractive Tableaux

THAT WILL BE PRESENTED DURING THE ACTION OF
THE DRAMA OF

THE FALL OF BABYLON.

Tableau I.

IS a truthful and strikingly magnificent representation of the incidents occurring in and about the City of Babylon while it was besieged by the troops of Cyrus, King of Persia, under the command of Darius, and during the interval between one of the unsuccessful attempts made by the Persians to enter the City by force, and its final capture by strategem.

THE GREAT WALL OF BABYLON.

The audience when assembled will be confronted with the massive wall surrounding the city, over and behind which will be seen the tops of the most prominent buildings brilliantly illuminated, as if by the early morning sunlight.

The guards on the wall and at the several towers are seemingly without fear of imminent danger, while the people from the surrounding country, with camels and other beasts of burden, are passing in and out of the center gate, carrying merchandise and provisions to the market within.

THE HUNTING PROCESSION.

After a number have paid toll and been permitted to enter, the announcement is made that the reigning Prince Belshazzar, accompanied by his body-guard and escort, are approaching the gate on their way out of the city to the favorite hunting grounds of the King. This necessarily causes all other persons to be delayed at the gate until after the royal party have passed, and in returning his gracious recognition the people bow in humble submission to their sovereign, after which the regular flow of travel is permitted, until some persons, evidently laboring under intense excitement, are seen hurriedly coming from the tower [right side] toward the gate, as if fleeing from impending danger and endeavoring by violent gestures to explain that hostile troops are approaching from that quarter.

ALARM AT THE GATES.

The guards on the wall, now thoroughly aroused, despite their fatigue after the night's vigil, are actively engaged in signaling for assistance and conveying the alarming intelligence that an attack is pending. The signals are repeated from tower to tower, and so on until the entire city is fully alarmed.

Immediately a trusty and fleet courier is dispatched in the direction taken by the King, in hopes that he may be overtaken and fully informed of impending danger.

The advance guard of the Persians now appear before the wall and after a brief skirmish move toward the center, followed by their comrades, continually making hostile demonstrations while advancing, until the entire front of the city is invested by them.

ATTACK ON THE CITY.

A general attack is now made, the archers and spearmen using their weapons with all the skill at their command, making it almost impossible for the Babylonian troops to expose themselves upon the walls.

The catapaults, flanked by additional archers, are now placed, and begin at once to hurl rocks and dreadful balls of fire into the unfortunate city, causing consternation and dismay to take possession of every one. Anon the battering ram is placed in front of the main gate, and herculean efforts are made to destroy the gate with this terrible engine of war, and thus effect an entrance into the city.

THE PERSIANS REPULSED.

While the greatest excitement prevails the Babylonian Prince suddenly appears, having nobly determined (as soon as he had received the warning sent him) to risk his own life, if necessary, in defense of his city and people. The most desperate hand-to-hand encounters occur; troops from the interior pass out of the gate to the assistance of the King; the battering ram is removed; Belshazzer engages the Persian general in mortal combat. The Persians are routed, and are finally driven around the tower out of sight.

Tableau 11.

REMOVAL OF THE WALL.

After an intermission (during which it is supposed that the fighting is continued on the other side of the city, and the Babylonians succeed in capturing the Persian General and some of the troops), the stupendous undertaking of removing the wall, that up to this time had stood between the audience and the city, will be begun, thus gradually disclosing to view the magnificent representation of

"BABYLON THE GREAT."

" The Beauty of the Chaldee's Excellency." The palace of Nabonadis in the center, apparently extending along the river for over three miles. On the left is the Tower of Babel; adjacent thereto the Temple of Belus, the shrine of the god Baal; on the right of the palace the embankment of the river Euphrates, with the steps leading down to the water's edge; the bridge

CHEWERS OF GUM

... WILL FIND ...

SMITH'S

"NATIONAL."—Flag Wrapper—Mint Flavor.

"YLANG YLANG."—In Japanese Willow Boxes.

"COUGH."—For Coughs, Colds and Bronchial Affections.

STRICTLY PURE AND FIRST-CLASS IN EVERY RESPECT.

For Sale by CONFECTIONERS, DRUGGISTS, and the Trade Generally.

. . MANUFACTURED BY . . .

H. D. Smith & Co. 56 and 58 Main St. *CINCINNATI, O.*

F. Szwirschina & Co.

Masquerade and Theatrical

COSTUMERS,

No. 390 VINE STREET, CINCINNATI, O.

This establishment has furnished all the costumes for the public processions, especially for the Order of Cincinnatus, during the seasons of 1882, 1883, 1884 and 1885, and for the Fall of Babylon, 1886, for Rome under Nero, 1887, and for Fall of Babylon, for 1888.

Costumers for the Order of Cincinnatus.

spanning the river, connecting the palace with the beautiful Hanging Gardens; further to the right the Temple of Beltis, all combining to make a picture that is so massive in its proportions, so complete in detail, so incomparable in its grandeur, that the opportunity presented at this time for its inspection should be taken advantage of by every one, so that a lasting impression may be had of this, *the grandest spectacle ever presented on any stage.*

INTERIOR OF THE CITY.

The people are seen upon the streets, some in groups waiting with breathless anxiety for news from the army, others more content, pursuing their daily avocations, when a solemn procession of Chaldean priests is seen emerging from the Temple of Belus, led by the high priest.

It is in the Book of Daniel that the Chaldean caste make their appearance most distinctly as the possessors not only of a special "learning," but of a peculiar "tongue." They are associated with the magicians, astrologers, sorcerers and soothsayers, probably classes of the Order. They are addicted especially to the art of divination and framed predictions of the future. They sought to avert evil and to insure good by purifications, sacrifices, and enchantments. They were versed in the arts of prophesying by means of the flight of birds, and of explaining dreams and prodigies, and omens furnished by the entrails of animals offered in sacrifice.

RELIGIOUS CEREMONIES OF THE CHALDEANS.

In accordance with their custom from time immemorial, to consult the gods upon all important occasions, they are now about to petition their deity for assistance in the present emergency, and burn incense while praying for the success of the Babylonian cause.

At the other end of the stage another group of priests is seen emerging from the Temple of Beltis, and are endeavoring to divine the future from the flight of birds, and finally march toward the palace preceded by their idols. Girls and children

BELL, MILLER & CO.,

IMPORTING RETAILERS.

RACE & SIXTH STS., CINCINNATI, O.

Silks, Dress Goods, Millinery,

*CLOAKS, SUITS, HOSIERY, GLOVES, DOMESTICS,
LACES, EMBROIDERIES AND*

MENS' FURNISHING GOODS.

Retailing at Wholesale Prices.   Visitors to the City cordially invited
to call upon us.

Bell, Miller & Co., Race & Sixth Sts.

8, 10 & 12 West Sixth Street, CINCINNATI, O.

bearing flowers also approach the palace, in the windows and corridors of which can be seen the Queen Nitocris and other ladies of the royal household, while in the lower apartments are seen the officers of the State, all anxiously awaiting news of the welfare of the King.

Suddenly, joyous sounds are heard in the north; shouts of victory become more distinct. The Chaldeans immediately give voice to their pent-up feelings by singing praises to their gods.

THE TRIUMPHAL PROCESSION:

All then move in the direction indicated by sounds of rejoicing as the place to meet the victors, and are overjoyed to see the King leading Persian prisoners through the streets of the city toward the palace. No restraint is placed upon the populace in their demonstrations of joy. Flowers are strewn in the pathway of the king by beautiful maidens. The Chaldeans chant a pean, the warriors marching to the martial music. Prisoners show their discomfiture, and are cruelly and brutally handled.

Slaves and concubines evince their joy by graceful movements in familiar dances.

The excitement is kept up without ceasing until the King retires to the Temple of Belus, and there performs the sacred rite of sacrificing a suckling on the golden altar devoted to that purpose, erected without the temple. As soon as he has performed this portion of his religious duty, he enters the temple to continue his devotions.

It having been proclaimed that this would be a day of rejoicing and feasting, arrangements had been made for the amusement of the populace, by having a vessel bring from one of the adjoining provinces a troupe of Egyptians, with dancing girls, snake charmers, acrobats, caged animals, and other attractions.

ARRIVAL OF THE AFRICANS

Upon the arrival of this vessel, and the embarkation of the passengers, the multitude are entertained by an exhibition of spear-throwing, dancing, feats of strength, and other demonstrations of their skill.

It now being the hour of sunset, when objects are not so easily distinguished, it is difficult to determine the exact nature of the procession that is seen approaching from the direction of the Tower of Babel, until, upon drawing nearer, it is seen to be the return of the bridegroom to his home, accompanied by his bride.

THE JEWISH WEDDING.

A beautiful custom was prevalent at this time, particularly among the Jews, when on the wedding day the bridegroom dressed in festive attire, with turban and crown, or garland, of gold, silver, roses, myrtle, or olive, according to his circumstances, highly perfumed, accompanied by his friends, preceded by musicians and singers, calls at the house of his bride, where she, robed in white, with veil covering her whole body, in token of submission, with her hair flowing, stands ready to receive him and accompany him to his home, while mutual friends are giving vent to audible expressions of gladness.

LAMENTATION OF THE JEWS BY THE RIVERS OF BABYLON.

At this time in the evening it was customary for the Jews to repair to the banks of the river and console themselves by singing some of their favorite songs, although they were somewhat in the form of a lamentation.

Being captives they were necessarily despondent, although only captives in name. They had become naturalized to their present homes, where their treatment was mild.

In Psalms cxxxvii., where the exiles pour out their griefs, the only complaint as to their treatment in captivity is that they were required to sing their native songs. •

The pathetic language of the Psalmody being: " By the rivers of Babylon there we sat down; yea, we wept when we remembered Zion, we hanged our harps on the willows in the midst thereof."

"For there they that carried us away captive *required of us a song;* and they that wasted us required of us mirth, saying, *Sing us one of the Songs of Zion.*"

CHORUS—BY THE RIVERS OF BABYLON.

עַל נַהֲרוֹת בָּבֶל נֵשֵׁב בָּדָד וְנִבְכֶּה:

w'nivke bodod ne'she'v bovel naharo's Al

עַל אֵלִּי עֶרְכָּה עִיר הַקּוֹדֶשׁ · אֵיךְ נָפְלָה מִשָּׁמַיִם לָאָרֶץ:

l'orez mishomajim nofalt e'ich hakodesh ir erko' e'le Al

שָׁפַּךְ יָהּ כָּאֵשׁ חֲמָתוֹ · נִלְקַדְתְּ בַּעֲוֹנֹתֵינוּ:

ba'wo'nosenu nilkadt chamo'so koe'sh Joh shofach

נִשְׂרַף הֵיכָלֵךְ · מַלְכֵּיךְ הָלַךְ שְׁבִי לִפְנֵי הַקּוֹרֶץ:

hakorez lifney shevi holach malkech becholoch Nisraf

יוֹשְׁבַיִךְ נֶאֱנָחִים בְּאֶרֶץ לֹא יָדְעוּ לֹא יָדְעוּ אֲבוֹתֵינוּ:

awo'senu jo'du lo jo'du lo be'e'rez ne'e'nochim joshwajich

אֲחַי! הַקֶּצֶף הַזֶּה יְהִי לְמָשָׁל לְדוֹרִים ·

le'do'rim le'mo'shol jehi ha'seh hakezef acha'j!

בַּל נֹאמַר אֶל הֵיכָל יָהּ בַּל יָרוּ הַמּוֹרִים · בַּל יָרוּ הַמּוֹרִים:

ha'morim jo'ro' bal ha'morim jo'ro' bal Joh hechol el nomar bal

As night has by this time encompassed the city with its sombre shadows, the Jews retire sorrowfully, thus bringing to a close the second part.

Tableau III.

The brilliant interior of the banquet hall of the Palace of Nabonadis, that has heretofore been concealed from the audience, by a curtain stretched across the opening on the side next

to them, will be disclosed to view, showing the female slaves arranging the decorations, and other slaves carrying the sacred vessels from the Temple of Belus to be used during the banquet and feast given in this place by Belshazzar.

THE SACRED VESSELS FROM JERUSALEM.

The Jews, seeing this sacreligious handling and use of these vessels that they had been taught to look upon with veneration and awe, are inclined to express their indignation by violent treatment of those who are seemingly responsible, but are restrained by Daniel, who advises them to control their feelings, and leave the just punishment of the offenders to the God of Israel, who had already inspired the prophets to predict their downfall and annihilation.

The King, having completed his devotions, is seen leaving the Temple of Belus and approaching the palace ; his pathway is lighted by torches, borne by his attendants.

The guests that have been invited to the feast are assembling, and upon the entrance of the King all arise to salute him in a manner appropriate to his exalted station. He motions all to be seated, and the banquet begins.

Belshazzar was determined to make this a memorable occasion, and, at the same time, show his indifference to the success of the Persians and their continued efforts to capture the city, relying upon the apparent impregnability of the walls, and the immense amount of provisions and supplies at his command, in addition to the enormous resources of the city itself.

THE FEAST OF BELSHAZZAR.

The King fully prepared to indulge his appetite for revelry and debauch, has instructed his officers to arrange a series of exhibitions for the amusement and edification of himself and guests during the progress of the feast. The strict discipline governing the guards surrounding the palace is relaxed upon this occasion, and the populace are permitted to draw near and view the sumptuous entertainment from the outside.

Following in rapid succession are exhibitions of skill in dancing by slaves, spear and sword exercise by warriors chosen from the King's personal guard, who are so expert in the use of their weapons, and so agile and graceful in their movements, as to command the most sincere and profound admiration of all who witness their exhibition of skill.

In marked contrast with the preceding, will be the peaceful gathering of the Jews and Chaldeans, who in obedience to the commands of the King, are assembled to assist in increasing the pleasures of the evening, by singing appropriate songs, in their own inimitable style.

BACCHANALIAN CHORUS.

לבלשאצר לבלשאצרל לבלשאצר: יקומו נא בי הצער

hazaar b'li no jokumu l'belsazar l'belsazar l'belsazar

כל אחי! הכוסות למלא, לשמח לבכם ·

libchem lesameach l'male hakosos achaj kol

וכל לשון יקרא את בעלה· ובלשאצר יתן שכרה:

sechoro jiten w'belsazar baalo es jekore loshon wechol

היין טהור מן ארצינו, יקום נא עם יין מן ארץ אחינו

achenu erez min jajin im no jokum ᴖzenu min tohor hajajin

למלא כום וכום ושותים לבלשאצר אליך שר השרים·

hasorim sar elecho l'belsazar w'shosim w'kos kos l'male

אכלו ושתו כל אחי· והיו תמיד שמח ·

ᴖomeach tomid w'h'ju achaj kol ushsu ichlu

ורעה לא היה עמנו: וקרא זה אל זה בקול רם,

rom b'kol se el se w'koro immonu hejeh lo w'rooh

לבלשאצר נתנו דברי שיר:

sh'r divre nitnu l'belsazar

יקומו נא בלי הצער כל אחי, הכוסות למלא

l'malle hakosos achaj kol hazaar b'li no jokumu

עם היין לשמח לבכם, וכל לשון יקרא את בעלה?

baalo es jekore loshon w'chol libchem lesameacn hajajin im

ובלשאצר יתן שכרה:

sechoro jiten w'belsazar

לכן תהי האמת נאדרת בהגישי לך זאת העטרת

hoateres sos lecho b'hagi·hi neederes hoemes tehi lochen

לענד ראשך בה · לכן אתם אלי כוסכם מלא אחי

achaj mole kos'chem jela atem lochen boh roshcho leaned

ותנו קול ושיר לבלשאצר לך אביר :

abir lecho l'belsazar w'shir kol usenu

יקומו נא בלי הצער כל אחי, הכוסות למלא

l'malle hakosos achaj kol hazaar b'li no jokumu

בהגישי לך זאת העטרה לענד ראשך בה ·

boh roshcho l'aned hoatoro sos lecho behagishi

לכן אתם אלי כוסכם מלא אחי

achaj mole kos'chem elaj atem lochen

ותנו קול ושיר לבלשאצר לך אביר :

abir lecho l'belsazar w'shir kol usenu

The King is now in that condition which is the result of
too frequent and intemperate indulgence in liquor, and fully
prepared for further excesses, so there need be no surprise at
his determination to publicly wound the feelings of the Jews
by a further desecration of the sacred vessels.

While, in obedience to his expressed wish, all are stand-
ing, prepared to drink in honor of the god Baal, they are
startled by the apparition of the

"HANDWRITING ON THE WALL."

Consternation and dismay are depicted upon every coun-
tenance; they are unable to understand the meaning of this
miraculous exhibition of divine power.

What can it mean? How can it be explained? Happy
thought! send for the Chaldeans, the spiritual advisers, whom

they have been taught to believe know all things, and can foretell the future.

Messengers are dispatched at once to the Temple of Belus for the high priest, *Rab Mag*, with the positive command "to repair at once to the Palace," *by order of the King.*

WARNING OF DANGER.

A mounted warrior approaches from the north tower, halting at one of the entrances to the palace, informs the officers that the Persians are gathering at the water gates of the city. He is treated scornfully and commanded to return to his post.

The Chaldean high priest and his associates *Ciden*, *Nabrianus*, and *Sudinius* arrive, and with an effort to appear self-possessed, and thus impress their auditors with a sense of superior knowledge, proceed to consult with one another as to the meaning of the phenomena, but their evasive answers prepare the King for their final admission that, to them, it is incomprehensible.

Queen Nitocris, remembering the fact that the Prophet Daniel had been called upon, under somewhat similar circumstances, to interpret a dream of Nebuchadnezzar's, and how successful he had been, pursuaded Belshazzer to send for Daniel. Accordingly a messenger is dispatched with instructions to have him appear forthwith.

DRAINING THE BED OF THE RIVER EUPHRATES.

Another courier appears and informs an officer that the Persians have succeeded in turning the channel of the river Euphrates and that even now the water is leaving the bed of the river exposed, as can readily be seen in that portion of it adjoining the palace.

This alarming intelligence is conveyed to Belshazzar, who, in a violent and excitable manner, declares that he will not be annoyed with receiving any more messages, under penalty of death to the person violating this order.

OUR ASSISTANTS.

SCENERY.—Designed and painted by . . . . . . JNO. RETTIG, Esq.

COSTUMES.—Designed by . . . . $\begin{cases} \text{WILHELM of London, Eng.,} \\ \text{F. SZWIRCHINA of Cincinnati.} \end{cases}$

EXECUTED BY . . . . $\begin{cases} \text{Miss FISHER of London, Eng.,} \\ \text{M. LANDORF of Paris,} \\ \text{F. SZWIRCHINA & CO. of Cincinnati.} \end{cases}$

CHORUSES.—Composed and directed by . . Prof. HERMAN GEROLD.

BABYLONIAN GUARDS.—By members of First Regiment O. N. G. under the command of Capt. W. G. SMITH and Lieut. ED. LOVEL.

THE TERPSICHOREAN REVELS.—Especially arranged and produced by . . . . Prof. C. L. W. GEYER.

THE MUSIC FOR THE BALLABILLE. $\begin{cases} \text{Prof. ADAM WEBER,} \\ \text{Prof. HERMAN GEROLD.} \end{cases}$
Expressly composed by

ORCHESTRA.—Under the direction of . . . . Prof. ADAM WEBER.

MECHANICAL EFFECTS.—By . . . . Mr. GEORGE FIELDS.

PROPERTIES.—By . . . . Mr. W. H. GUNN.

ARMOUR.—By . . . . Mr. H. IMBUS.

USHERS. . . . $\begin{cases} \text{Under the direction of the \textit{Social Committee of the Order}} \\ \textit{of Cincinnatus} \text{ and W. E. STEWART and Assistants.} \end{cases}$

POLICE.—In command of . . . . Capt. WM. F. HAZEN.

THE PROPHET DANIEL.

Daniel appears, calm, dignified and saintly in appearance, relying upon divine assistance. Instantly he realizes the presence of Omnipotence, and without hesitation proceeds to interpret the mystic meaning:

"MENE, NENE, TEKEL, UPHARSIN."

"THOU HAST BEEN WEIGHED IN THE BALANCE AND FOUND WANTING."

Before the revelers have had time to recover from their fright, the Persians are upon them, having entered the city upon the dry bed of the river and through the water gates to the very precincts of the palace.

SLAUGHTER BY PERSIANS.

Now begins an indescribable scene of slaughter, carnage, and destruction. From palace and castle, from gate and tower, through the broad avenues, along the by-ways, a surprised and terrified people flee, but only to be overtaken and slain by their cruel pursuers. "Every one that is found shall be thrust through, and every one that is joined unto them shall fall by the sword."

To this indiscriminate slaughter of the inhabitants, Xenophon testifies, and to restrain his soldiers therein, Cyrus commanded them to massacre only those found in the streets, while to the people he issued an order to remain within their houses.

DEATH OF BELSHAZZAR—BURNING OF THE CITY.

Still imbued with the idea that he is invincible, Belshazzar, in an inebriated condition, advances to meet Darius, the Persian General, in a brief but one-sided and fatal encounter, for "in that night was Belshazzar, the King of the Chaldeans, slain." This tragic event, in connection with the realistic representation of portions of the city in flames, and falling buildings, is a fitting climax to this unique and magnificent entertainment.

Programme.

—OVERTURE.—

I.

1st.   Entrance of merchants and peasants to the city.
2nd.   King's hunting party.
3rd.   Attack on city by Persians.
4th.   Grand Battle Scene.—Defeat of Persians.

INTERMISSION,   -   10 MINUTES.

II.

1st.   Removal of walls, disclosing Babylon the Great.
2nd.   Jewish Wedding Procession.
3rd.   Chorus of Chaldean Priests at Temple of Belus.
4th.   Greeting to Victory Procession.
5th.   Grand Procession of Victory.
6th.   King and Retinue retire to Temple to offer sacrifice.
7th. }   Entertainment for the People of Babylon in honor of victory over
8th. }   the Persians.
9th.   Lamentation of the Jews by the Waters of Babylon.

III.

1st.   King and Retinue from Temple of Belus to Palace with seven
      armed candelabra and sacred vessals.
2nd.   Interior of Palace.—The Feast of Belschazzar.
3rd.   Grand Terpsichorean Revels by the Dancing Girls of Babylon.
4th.   Handwriting on the Wall.
5th.   Draining of the River Euphrates.—Attack by Persians.—The
      destruction and Fall of Babylon.

ALMS & DOEPKE,

Wholesale and Retail Dealers in Staple ond Fancy Dry Goods, Carpets, etc.

MAIN, CANAL AND HUNT STREETS.

Our coaches are now running down Main to Fifth, west on Fifth to Walnut, to Fourth, and west to Race, north on Race to Ninth, to Main, and to the store.

www.ingramcontent.com/pod-product-compliance
Lightning Source LLC
Chambersburg PA
CBHW021444090426
42739CB00009B/1636